IT'S NEVER OKAY TO BORROW SOMEONE ELSE'S TOOTHBRUSH

Also by Richard Grady

One Day Ahead: A Tour de France Misadventure

Distinctly Average Entrepreneur

IT'S NEVER OKAY TO BORROW SOMEONE ELSE'S TOOTHBRUSH

Richard Grady

Copyright © Richard Grady 2016
www.richardgrady.co.uk
Twitter: @mr_richardgrady
Facebook: facebook.com/richardgradywrites

Richard Grady has asserted his right under the Copyright, Designs and Patents Act 1988 to be identified as the author of this work.

This book is copyright material and is sold subject to the condition that it must not be copied, reproduced, transferred, distributed, leased, licensed or publicly performed or used in any way except as specifically permitted in writing by the author, as allowed under the terms and conditions under which it was purchased or as strictly permitted by applicable copyright law. Any unauthorised distribution or use of this text may be a direct infringement of the author's rights and those responsible may be liable in law accordingly.

First published in Great Britain by
Shore Publishing 2016
www.shorepublishing.co.uk

ISBN 978-0-9543736-3-4

For
Emily, Isabelle,
Archie & Olivia

Author's Note

As an adult who, naturally, knows best, there is nothing I like more than to impart little gems of wisdom to my nieces and nephew. They love being educated by their uncle: 'Tell us more Uncle Richard, teach us to be better humans!' they shout.

Of course they don't. Just like children the world over, they already know everything and I am far too old to have anything worthwhile to say. Well, that's where you are wrong kids! Here are 534 nuggets of genius which will help you lead a better life!!

Richard Grady

It's more important to enjoy your job than to earn a lot of money.

It's better to live in the worst house on the best street than the best house on the worst street.

Get into the habit of exercising regularly.

Respect all living things.

It's Never Okay to Borrow…

Look at the stars.

Own a pet before you have a child. If you find looking after the pet is a pain you are in no way ready for kids.

Never buy a brand new car. Let someone else suffer the initial hit of depreciation and get one a couple of years old instead.

Everything is negotiable.

...*Someone Else's Toothbrush*

Don't leave your wheelie bin out in the street once it has been emptied. It's messy.

Invent something.

Learn DIY skills. If you then prefer to employ trades people, at least you'll know when they are trying to rip you off.

Go on a first aid course and repeat it every few years.

It's Never Okay to Borrow…

When selling a property, use an online service to advertise and then handle the viewings yourself. No one knows your home and its good points better than you do.

Don't go to sleep on an argument.

If your partner doesn't add to your life, you are with the wrong partner.

...Someone Else's Toothbrush

No to B.O.

Own a bike
(but stay off the roads).

Try skiing at least once.

Understand what your means
are and live within them.

*You don't need to keep
up with the Joneses.*

It's Never Okay to Borrow…

When driving assume that every other road user is about to do something stupid.

Treat yourself to an afternoon nap on occasion.

If you fancy a break at work, offer to make everyone a cup of tea or coffee. Your colleagues will appreciate it and you'll get a little rest in the kitchen.

...Someone Else's Toothbrush

Park at the rear of car parks. The extra walking is good for you and there is less chance of someone scratching your car.

Allow yourself a pyjama day from time to time.

Don't waste money on rent if you can help it. Live with mum and dad for as long as you/they can bear it and then buy your own place.

Keep a charging cable for your phone in the car.

It's Never Okay to Borrow…

Understand how to check your car's oil/water levels and tyre pressures and then do it weekly.

Build a gingerbread house at Christmas.

Never drive around with your car windows down and music blaring. You will be the only one who thinks you look cool.

Work your socks off in your twenties and thirties and give yourself the option of winding down sooner rather than later.

...Someone Else's Toothbrush

There is no reason for any male to walk around the town with their shirt off regardless of how hot it is. Topless is for the beach and the garden.

Girls: Tell your friend if she has something stuck in her teeth.

Boys: Don't bother, it's funnier to leave it there.

Do voluntary work at some point in your life.

It's Never Okay to Borrow…

Girls: Never let your friend go out in public looking like a bag of rags.

Boys: The above does not apply - let them wear what they like and enjoy it knowing that they'll do the same for you one day.

If your partner doesn't make you laugh, you are with the wrong partner.

If you don't make your partner laugh, perhaps they are with the wrong partner.

...Someone Else's Toothbrush

It's never too late to change career and find something better.

It's never okay to borrow someone else's toothbrush.

Friends will drift in and out of your life. This is fine; don't feel pressured to keep in touch with everyone forever.

Maintaining true friendships is effortless.

It's Never Okay to Borrow…

Spend a day watching a box set in one hit.

Please don't pierce your face. Ideally, just stick to earrings but seriously, whatever else you do, stay away from your face!

Drinking alcohol won't make you a good karaoke singer…
…neither will it improve your dancing.

...Someone Else's Toothbrush

Tattoos will go out of fashion. Don't be stuck with one when they do.

See the world while you are young. The older you get, the less bothered you'll be...
...plus the travel insurance will be dearer.

When you are old and grey, you'll regret the things you didn't do more than the things you did.

It's Never Okay to Borrow…

Learn to play a musical instrument.

Chances are, in twenty years time, you'll have completely different friends to those you have now bar one or two.

Everything you do online leaves a 'footprint'. Do you really want a future employer to see pictures of you drinking shots until you are sick?

...Someone Else's Toothbrush

Watch 'Ferris Bueller's Day Off'.

Spend time playing outdoors - whatever age you are.
Housework will wait.

Find books you enjoy and immerse yourself in them.

Appreciate your parents. They'll do anything for you, forgive you without question and love you unconditionally.
Make them proud.

It's Never Okay to Borrow…

Make the effort to speak the local language when abroad.

Find a good plumber, electrician, builder and mechanic and keep a note of their contact details to hand.

Be prepared to complain about poor service but do it politely.

It's never too early to start looking after your skin.

...Someone Else's Toothbrush

```
Enjoy a sunset and a
sunrise from a beach.

Enjoy a sunset and a
sunrise from a mountain.
```

When you are out and about,
make sure your loved ones
know you are okay.
Take time to check in.

You own possessions
but if you aren't careful,
they can also own you.

It's Never Okay to Borrow…

Think twice before posting anything on social media. Once it's out there, it's out there forever. If you wouldn't be happy to show Great Grandma, keep it to yourself.

Own a decent pair of binoculars.

I know you think you know everything but you don't. You will <u>*always*</u> be learning.

Chips and cheese - yum!

...Someone Else's Toothbrush

Read 'To Kill a Mockingbird' and then watch the film.

Quality is remembered long after the price is forgotten.

If something is worrying you, consider whether it will be an issue in a year's time. If not, stop worrying. If it will be, then deal with it.

Don't be afraid to ask for help.

It's Never Okay to Borrow…

See your favourite group or singer live.

Learn to swim.

It's okay to burp but not in public and it's probably best not to tell Nana.

*Hugs are good.
Be a hugger.*

Don't eat yellow snow.

...Someone Else's Toothbrush

In an empty house a radio is great company.

It doesn't matter what you do to earn an honest living as long as you do something.

Working hard at school will give you more opportunities.
You don't have to become a brain surgeon but it's nice to have the option.

It's Never Okay to Borrow…

Take a year off.

If you ever get the chance to do any kind of reality TV show, say 'no'.

It's good to know what is going on in the world but most news reported in the media is bad and will depress you.
Find a balance.

Look after your teeth.

...Someone Else's Toothbrush

Telling someone bad news by text isn't acceptable.

Your wedding day won't be the best day of your life but it could be the most expensive…
…unless you get divorced.
Choose carefully.

If you and a friend are chased by a bear remember, you don't need to out run the bear, you only need to out run your friend.

It's Never Okay to Borrow…

You don't have to be in a relationship - being single is okay too.

Never trust a dog to guard your food.

Prunes. No.

You don't always need to aim for perfection. Sometimes 'good enough' is good enough.

...Someone Else's Toothbrush

Watch 'The Sting'.

If you want a kitten, start by asking for a horse.

Make mistakes but learn from them.

Smoking.
Not big. Or clever.

Pay bills on time.

It's Never Okay to Borrow…

Take lots of photos but don't miss out because you are taking lots of photos. Enjoy events through your own eyes rather than a camera lens.

If it tastes sweet it probably isn't very good for you.

Salad and vegetables aren't just 'decoration for the plate'. Eat both!

...Someone Else's Toothbrush

Take time to chat to restaurant waiting staff. Most people won't give them the time of day.

People in pubs don't give good stock market tips.

Snorkel around a Maldivian island.

Carry a donor card.

It's Never Okay to Borrow…

If you 'think' you want to buy something but aren't completely sure, leave it a week and see how you feel. There's a good chance the novelty will have worn off.

New technology will almost always be cheaper a few months after it is first released.

The easiest way to lose weight is to buy bigger clothes but be warned, it's a slippery slope.

...Someone Else's Toothbrush

'12345' is NOT a good password...
...neither is 'password'.

Ironing is over-rated. A good shake will do.

A conversation is a two-way thing. Don't just talk about yourself and what you've been doing. Ask the other person questions and listen to their answers.

It's Never Okay to Borrow...

A gut reaction will often be the right one.

Take your shoes off when you enter someone else's house.

It's much better to be five minutes early than five minutes late. Be known for being on time.

Read documents carefully before signing them.

...Someone Else's Toothbrush

Don't have your stag/hen party the night before your wedding day.

Challenge yourself. Physically and mentally.

Back up your important computer files regularly. You WILL need the backup at some point, I guarantee it.

```
Don't put your feet on
the seats on a train.
```

It's Never Okay to Borrow…

Make a note of a good idea when you have it. Chances are, if you don't, you'll forget it.

When you check into a hotel make sure you know how to get out in an emergency.

The cheapest quote may not always be the best.

Keep a diary.

...Someone Else's Toothbrush

When negotiating a deal, always leave a suck in the orange for the other party.

Be honest.

It's okay to be wrong.

When guests leave your home, stand at the door and wave them off.

It's Never Okay to Borrow…

Make your partner laugh every day.

You can freeze milk.

Know where the stopcock in your home is and ensure it works.

There's nothing wrong with having the occasional alcoholic drink but if you can do without it, you'll save a small fortune over your lifetime.
Plus you will be healthier.

...Someone Else's Toothbrush

Take the stairs.

Fly with just carry-on luggage whenever possible.

Return everything you borrow.

Donate old clothes to charity.

Talk less. Listen more.

It's Never Okay to Borrow…

Be kind.

You'll probably have to do a job you hate at some point so do your best to get decent exam results so that at least you'll be getting well paid for doing it.

Remember your manners.

Understand and accept that life isn't fair.

...Someone Else's Toothbrush

Know when to keep your opinion to yourself.

Get to know your neighbours.

Learn the difference between 'there', 'their' and 'they're'.

Learn the difference between 'your' and 'you're'.

Hang washing outside to dry whenever it's warm enough.

It's Never Okay to Borrow…

The novelty of a new car wears off in a matter of weeks but will cost you hundreds or even thousands of pounds.

Fresh air won't kill you.

Always have a tissue in your pocket or handbag.

Rich Tea biscuits are the best for dunking.
Or Hobnobs. You can't go wrong with a Hobnob.

...Someone Else's Toothbrush

Put the toilet seat down.

Always look after trades people with tea and biscuits but don't go overboard or they'll never finish the work.

Aim to be a better parent than your parents.
(I'm not saying your parents are bad, I'm saying do even better!)

It's Never Okay to Borrow…

Be patient with learner drivers.

When selling your house or car, if someone tries to knock the price down, don't focus on the discount, focus on the money you'll be getting.

Never start a sentence with, 'I'm not being funny but…'

Never finish a sentence with, 'Yeah?'

...Someone Else's Toothbrush

You can go almost anywhere you want if you wear a hi-viz jacket, carry a clipboard and look serious.

Singing whilst wearing headphones is never a good look.

You'll be judged by the company you keep.

'Lol', 'OMG' and 'Gr8' are not words.

It's Never Okay to Borrow…

Waste time wisely. It's precious.

When using public toilets, always check for toilet paper first.

Don't dry clothes on the radiator.

When walking two abreast on the pavement, don't expect people coming the other way to walk into the road to go around you.

...Someone Else's Toothbrush

```
Wake up, be awesome,
  go back to sleep.
```

If you are about to say something mean about someone, make sure they aren't standing behind you.

Never trust anyone with more than two mobile phones.

Laugh uncontrollably.

It's Never Okay to Borrow…

Watch 'Bugsy Malone'.

Pleasing everyone is impossible. Annoying everyone is much easier. Be aware.

It's better to keep quiet and let everyone think you are a fool than to speak and let them know it.

Everyone likes a person who gets to the point quickly.

...Someone Else's Toothbrush

When you start shouting, you've lost the argument.

Don't waste time looking at weather forecasts. They are often wrong and you can't do anything about it anyway.

Don't borrow money on credit cards - it is far too expensive. Ideally, don't borrow money at all other than a mortgage.

Be organised.

It's Never Okay to Borrow…

If you find work you really love, the chances are that you'll have more fun, more freedom and more money if you work for yourself rather than someone else.

If you aren't happy single you won't be happy in a relationship.

Use the 'snooze' button.

If you say, 'Don't take this the wrong way but…' you can be sure that they will take it the wrong way.

...Someone Else's Toothbrush

Open windows.

No one is interested in another of your selfies.

People on Facebook and Twitter don't care what you are having for dinner.

If you want to end a text conversation, simply reply with 'Haha'.

It's Never Okay to Borrow…

Offer to call telemarketers back when they are at home later that evening.

Keep carrier bags in the boot of your car.

Recycle.

Autocorrect is sometimes wrong.

...Someone Else's Toothbrush

ALWAYS re-read texts, emails and letters before sending them.

Don't send an angry email or text in the heat of the moment. Type it and then sleep on it.

Never be tempted to experiment with a moustache.

If you see a 'wet paint' sign, don't touch to check.

It's Never Okay to Borrow…

Most of the things you will worry about will never happen.

Call your parents.

Aim to clear your mortgage as soon as possible. Mortgages keep people at work. You can live pretty cheaply once you own your house.

Sit outside at a coffee shop and people watch.

...Someone Else's Toothbrush

```
Don't drink too much
   at work events.
```

Actually, don't drink too much full-stop!

Never say, 'Blue sky thinking' or 'Let's think outside of the box'.

Bright red lipstick is never a good idea.

It's Never Okay to Borrow…

Give taxi drivers a decent tip. And waiting staff. But only if they are polite and give you good service.

Get a dashcam for your car.

Know where to use an apostrophe.

Learn the difference between 'lose' and 'loose'.

...Someone Else's Toothbrush

Read 'A Christmas Carol' in December and then watch the film (any adaptation).

Pay into a pension sooner rather than later.
Old age creeps up on you faster than you think.

Don't be the person who tells one joke after another.

A film you love is like an old friend. Enjoy it on a rainy day.

It's Never Okay to Borrow…

Even if you read a book every week, you will only have time to read a few thousand in your lifetime. There are millions of books out there so don't waste time on one you aren't enjoying.

Smile at shop assistants before they smile at you.

Read 'The Lion, the Witch and the Wardrobe'.

Smile more.

...Someone Else's Toothbrush

Make eye contact with people when talking to them. But don't stare. There's a fine line between friendly and polite and weird and scary.

Tip your hairdresser - he/she has significant control over your happiness.

Own a decent pair of sunglasses. Not only will they protect your eyes, they look cool too!

It's Never Okay to Borrow…

Boys: Always double-check your trouser zip is done up after using the bathroom.

Girls : Always check your dress isn't tucked into your underwear after using the bathroom…
…and make sure you don't have toilet paper stuck to your shoe.

Try lots of different hobbies.

```
Buy a random magazine
  from time to time and
read it. This will help
   you to converse on a
    variety of different
         subjects.
```

...Someone Else's Toothbrush

Know the procedure for going through airport security so that you don't hold up the people behind you.

Own a first aid kit.

With great power comes great responsibility (although this is probably only relevant if you become a superhero or the Prime Minister).

Learn some sign language.

It's Never Okay to Borrow…

No one on their death bed ever wished they had spent more time at work (or on Facebook or Twitter).

Declutter regularly.

Watch the original 'Star Wars' trilogy (don't bother with the newer ones).

Enjoy completing a jigsaw puzzle once in a while. The works of Jan van Haasteren are fun and challenging.

...Someone Else's Toothbrush

Before leaving a negative review online, consider whether you would make the same comment face to face with the recipient.

Learn the difference between 'to', 'too' and 'two'.

Be a bit cynical.

Dress for the job you want not the job you've got.

It's Never Okay to Borrow…

Never get into an argument on social media.

If someone is rude or angry towards you, remember that they might just be having a really bad day. Or they might just be rude and angry.

Don't talk to strangers online - they may not be who they say they are.

Aim to inspire.

...Someone Else's Toothbrush

Keep your school reports.

Give blood.

Tinder is not a good place to find a husband/wife.

You don't know better than the washing label instructions on your clothes.

It's Never Okay to Borrow…

Never buy an item of clothing which says 'Hand Wash Only' or 'Dry Clean Only'.

Own a dictionary.

Know where north, south, east and west are.

Remember people's names and use them.

Do what you love.

...Someone Else's Toothbrush

Get a window cleaner and always make him a cup of tea when he calls.

Keep a paper address book as a backup to any electronic records.

```
Vote but understand
what you are voting
for. Picking someone
    because he/she
 'looks nice' isn't
    good enough.
```

It's Never Okay to Borrow…

Drink water.

When you do stuff, stuff happens. So do stuff.

Clean up as you go.

Read 'Aesop's Fables'.

When you come across a word you don't understand take a moment to look it up.

...Someone Else's Toothbrush

Have a firm handshake.

The freedom money in the bank gives you means you get value from it even if you never spend it.

When you find a hobby you enjoy, get good at it.

Don't burn bridges. Whether it is work, relationships or something else, part on good terms as you never know when you might need to go back.

It's Never Okay to Borrow…

Take the time to compliment people.

```
Download airline
boarding cards to your
phone but always have
a paper copy too, just
       in case.
```

Keep some small change in the car for parking.

Don't believe everything you read online or watch on the news.

...Someone Else's Toothbrush

If you live a simpler life you can work considerably less. It's your choice.

Be excited by change.

It's okay to fail and it's better to fail than not to try in the first place.

Don't make decisions when you are angry or upset.

It's Never Okay to Borrow…

Alcohol + online shopping = a bad idea.

It's fine to put ice cream sprinkles on your cereal.

Your phone battery will last much longer if you don't check it so often.

Always make sure you are insured before driving someone else's car.

...Someone Else's Toothbrush

Don't be afraid to ask questions if you don't understand.

When someone asks you to be honest with them, they don't always want you to be honest with them.

Spend an afternoon watching the 'Back to the Future' trilogy.

Read 'The Curious Incident of the Dog in the Night-Time'.

It's Never Okay to Borrow…

```
Never heckle a
comedian. Remember,
it's their job to make
   you look stupid.
     You'll lose.
```

Never wear polka dot underwear beneath a white skirt.

Superhero boxer shorts stop being cool when you are about 9 years old.

...Someone Else's Toothbrush

Replace the cap after using a tube of toothpaste.

Even if someone promises not to tell anyone your secret, chances are that they will tell at least one other person.

Write a will.

Eat less sugar.

It's Never Okay to Borrow…

The person with final say on which movie to watch on Sky is the one who pays the bill.

Watch any Disney film.

Buy the best bed you can afford.

Never ask a woman when her baby is due unless you are absolutely certain that she is pregnant.

...Someone Else's Toothbrush

When you make a promise, keep it.

Be known for being reliable.

Always let people know if you are going to be late for an appointment - even if it is only by 10 minutes.

Always haggle when buying a car or a house.

It's Never Okay to Borrow…

Fit a safe in your home and use it.

Learn to say 'no'. You can't do everything for everyone.

Learn to say 'yes'. You never know where it might take you.

Make sure your home has smoke detectors and a carbon monoxide alarm and change the batteries annually.

...Someone Else's Toothbrush

It's not all about you - let other people have their moment in the spotlight.

Women generally don't like being given kitchen equipment as birthday presents.

Men generally love being given tools as birthday presents. Especially if they run on petrol.

It's Never Okay to Borrow…

Don't litter.

Play board games with your family.

When you have children buy them a trampoline. Get the biggest one you can afford.

Don't choose a job because of the salary. Choose a job because it's something you want to do.

...Someone Else's Toothbrush

Think carefully before you speak. Once you've said it, you can't take it back.

Aim to have multiple streams of income.

Keep a file of receipts for electrical products. They will be easily located if you ever need to claim under the warranty.

Bake a cake.
And then eat it!

It's Never Okay to Borrow…

Never start to decorate before covering your carpet and furniture with dust sheets - you will always spill paint if you do.

Always have an extra £20 in your wallet/purse just in case.

Own a toasted sandwich maker.

Never buy a car in the dark.

…Someone Else's Toothbrush

```
Spend an afternoon
with a beekeeper -
bees are fascinating
    creatures.
```

Never place your phone on the table in a coffee shop or restaurant. It is too easy for a thief to distract you and steal it.

Be cautious when connecting to public WiFi networks. Ideally, use your mobile 4G data when out as this is more secure.

It's Never Okay to Borrow…

Remember, a bargain is only a bargain if you were going to purchase the item in the first place.

```
Treat yourself to a
cooked breakfast on
   Sunday mornings.
```

When something happens which appears to be bad, it's often too early to tell if it's actually good.

...Someone Else's Toothbrush

Facebook is not the place to write about how you feel all of the time. That's what a diary is for.

Life always offers you a second chance. It's called 'tomorrow'.

Chocolate comes from cocoa, which is a tree. That makes it a plant. Chocolate is therefore salad.

It's Never Okay to Borrow…

When you need legal advice please ask a solicitor, not Facebook.

If you ever live in an apartment, aim to be on the top floor.

Stay away from debt.

When buying a home, don't lose a property you love for the sake of a few thousand pounds. You'll soon forget about the extra cost once you move in.

...Someone Else's Toothbrush

Don't let dried ketchup build up around the bottle cap. Wipe it clean after you use it. Same for toothpaste.

Never have any home improvement work carried out by someone who has knocked on your door touting for business.

Instead of keeping photos on your phone, have a few printed and display them in a frame.

It's Never Okay to Borrow…

Always check your change.

There will always be people who won't see your point of view.

Never complain about the food or the service in a restaurant if you aren't paying the bill.

Ride on a steam train.

...Someone Else's Toothbrush

If you are ever travelling and pass a 'Little Chef' restaurant, stop and eat. They do the best all day breakfasts!

Remember that DIY jobs will always take longer than you initially expect.

When experiencing bad times remember that 'this soon shall pass'. Unfortunately, the rule also applies to good times. Accept that life is a series of ups and downs.

It's Never Okay to Borrow…

Don't buy branded painkillers, cold relief medication or antihistamine. Own brands contain the same drugs but are considerably cheaper.

Learn how to complete a Rubik's Cube. It's easier than you think.

Never cycle in flip-flops.

If you do anything that puts you in the public eye, be prepared for some people to criticise you.

...Someone Else's Toothbrush

Teach others your skills.

Enter a sporting challenge event.

Don't be tempted to taste strawberry-scented shower gel (or any other 'flavour' for that matter).

You don't need a massive television.

It's Never Okay to Borrow…

Own a sewing kit and learn how to use it for basic repairs.

Keep some old clothes for gardening and DIY.

Never buy a home without some outside space. Even if it is just a balcony.

Always have a backup plan.

...Someone Else's Toothbrush

Enjoy the atmosphere of a live sporting event but know that you'll see far more by watching it on the television.

Don't try to force your opinion onto someone.

Life is a game. Play well but always play fair.

It's Never Okay to Borrow…

Don't fist bump or high five the person interviewing you for a job.

The world as you know it was created by the generations who went before you. Respect your elders - they are incredibly wise.

Find a mug you really like and use it for your first hot drink of the day.

...Someone Else's Toothbrush

Learn to read a map.

Have a favourite restaurant and get to know the manager and staff. They'll make you feel like a VIP every time you visit.

Mum and dad don't care that you have learnt the phone number of Childline off by heart. You still need to do what you are told.

It's Never Okay to Borrow…

Take an evening class.

Don't get sucked into TV soaps – you'll waste hours of your life every week.

Good people sometimes do bad things. Give second chances but think hard about giving a third.

Learn to find pleasure in simple things and you'll never be bored.

...Someone Else's Toothbrush

Buy a good quality pair of running trainers and use them for walking.

Write 'to do' lists and enjoy the process of ticking off completed jobs.

```
Never buy an exercise
   bike or a running
machine - you'll soon
get bored. Go outside
and exercise instead.
```

It's Never Okay to Borrow…

Don't take a short cut across someone's front garden (or rear garden for that matter).

Own a globe.

Whenever your parents tell you off it's because they are trying to make you a better person. How nice is that?!

Don't eat food from a knife.

...Someone Else's Toothbrush

Don't leave your keys near the front door. A sneaky thief could hook them through the letterbox.

Read anything by Roald Dahl.

Allow yourself time to be brilliant. If you spend your life working all hours for someone else, you'll never have time to develop your amazing ideas.

It's Never Okay to Borrow…

Build a sandcastle.

There's no substitute for knowing.

Never buy a house from someone you don't like.

Don't kill spiders - if you don't want them in the house, catch and release!

...Someone Else's Toothbrush

Don't leave mobile devices charging unattended.

Never leave your dishwasher or washing machine running when you go out.

```
Don't interrupt and
   don't talk over
      people.
```

It's 'everything' and 'anything' not 'everythink' and 'anyfink'.

It's Never Okay to Borrow…

Ice-skating is a fun way of combining enjoyment with pain.

Texting is the perfect way to miscommunicate how you feel and to misinterpret what other people mean.

Face problems and deal with them. Things won't necessarily just 'work themselves out'.

...Someone Else's Toothbrush

Don't walk and text.

In the unfortunate event of a fire, get out of the building before you Tweet about it.

Never trust anyone who puts the milk in before the cereal.

People often think an idea is ridiculous. Until it works. Then it's genius. Don't be put off from trying by the negativity of others.

It's Never Okay to Borrow…

You'll get everything you want in life if you lower your expectations.

Never test the depth of a river with both feet.

Experience is everything. Take advice from people who have actually experienced the problems you are facing.

...Someone Else's Toothbrush

The driver of the car always gets to pick the music.

Luck can be manufactured.

Don't knock an idea you can't improve upon.

Watch 'Chitty Chitty Bang Bang'.

It's Never Okay to Borrow…

Beware of monthly subscription charges – you'll soon forget about them but that won't stop them being deducted from your bank account.

The legal order of possession of the television remote control in a home is: father, mother, first child to grab it.

Read anything by Enid Blyton.

...Someone Else's Toothbrush

The best way to call a family meeting is to turn the WiFi router off and wait in that room.

Become an expert at something.

There's always an easy way or a hard way. The easy way won't always be the best way.

It's Never Okay to Borrow…

Learn to read between the lines.

When someone tells you a business idea won't work, consider what experience the person has in business themselves before deciding whether to listen.

Do not confuse your career with your life.

...Someone Else's Toothbrush

```
   No matter what
happens, someone will
find a way of taking
   it too seriously.
```

Everyone thinks they are a good driver.

Not everyone is a good driver.

In business, it is often the senior members of staff who earn the most money yet do the least work. Make the effort to be senior.

It's Never Okay to Borrow…

Common sense is not that common.

Everyone has a 'get rich quick' scheme that won't work.

Always be wary of looking after someone else's pet when it is close to its average life expectancy.

Go on a cruise.

...Someone Else's Toothbrush

When assembling flat pack furniture, you will always have pieces left over.

If an item of clothing says 'one size fits all', it won't fit anyone.

Work expands to fill the allotted time.

Watch anything directed by Stephen Spielberg.

It's Never Okay to Borrow…

If you are feeling down, watch 'Spandy Andy' on YouTube – guaranteed to provide a lift in spirits.

When exercising, if you're not pulling an ugly face, you're not working hard enough.

If you must gamble, be the bookie and be good at it.

Learn how to remove a tick safely.

...Someone Else's Toothbrush

If you must have a blog, make sure you have something worthwhile to say.

If an estate agent describes a property as being 'open plan', it means you will find the kitchen in the lounge.

Don't worry if you don't know what you want to be when you leave school. I'm 47 and I'm still not sure.

It's Never Okay to Borrow...

Using the word 'like' incorrectly and too frequently is incredibly annoying. As in, 'I was, like, so happy and like, so surprised'.

Using the word 'like' to describe something you said is even worse. As in, 'I was like, "I didn't do that!"' You said it, you didn't like it.

Visit any of the Disney theme parks.

...Someone Else's Toothbrush

You will eventually turn into your parents. You'll say the things that they say and do the things that they do. Don't fight it. It's inevitable.

Don't leave a voicemail message that is longer than 30 seconds.

Develop a cool signature - it'll be with you for life.

```
Avoid procrastination
 - just get it done!
```

It's Never Okay to Borrow…

Set goals and targets. How will you achieve your potential if you don't know what you are aiming for?

Try something new as often as you can.

Learn and understand the 'Pareto Principle' - the 80/20 rule.

There's always a way.

...Someone Else's Toothbrush

Analyse your weaknesses and work to improve them.

Take educated risks but don't 'bet the farm' on one thing however great you think it is. A 99% chance of success still has a risk of failure.

Nothing good ever happens after 2am.

Watch the box set of 'Fawlty Towers'.

It's Never Okay to Borrow…

Never judge a book by its movie.

```
    History constantly
  repeats itself. If you
  know what happened in
  the past, you'll have a
  good chance of knowing
  how a similar situation
   will play out in the
           future.
```

There's no substitute for having it in writing.

...Someone Else's Toothbrush

If you turn up and a sign says 'full body armour must be worn' it's probably best to give it a miss.

Don't be the fall guy - you want people laughing with you not at you.

It takes a wise man to be a fool but not all fools are wise.

It's Never Okay to Borrow…

If someone starts a sentence with, 'This is a very interesting story...' you can be sure that it won't be.

It's okay to be known for being careful with money but don't be known for being tight.

Own a good quality electric toothbrush.

Own a cool hat.

...Someone Else's Toothbrush

Overnight success usually takes many years to achieve.

The anticipation of buying something will often give you more pleasure than actually owning it.

```
If someone says
'but' halfway through
a sentence, you can
safely ignore the
first half of the
sentence.
```

It's Never Okay to Borrow...

Contrary to what they may say, no one is really interested in seeing all of your holiday photos.

Your partner should be someone you can enjoy doing nothing with.

Remember that a sales person will always have their own interests ahead of yours.

...Someone Else's Toothbrush

Get competitive quotes for your car and home insurance before renewing your cover each year.

Do the same for your phone, broadband and packaged TV contracts.

Always have breakdown cover for your car.

It's Never Okay to Borrow…

Buy someone a gift for absolutely no reason.

When someone says, 'No offence but…' they mean that what they are going to say is going to offend you but you can't get upset because they said 'no offence'.

It's better to get up early than to go to bed late.

...Someone Else's Toothbrush

```
When abroad, try
the local food.
```

Fold a Post-It note in half and
stick it to the wall before drilling
a hole. It will catch the dust.

Read 'Animal Farm' by
George Orwell.

Sometimes, not getting
what you want will turn
out to be far better.

It's Never Okay to Borrow…

Push yourself out of your comfort zone regularly.

When travelling, pack less stuff.

Consider turning a hobby into a business.

Find ways of generating passive income (income which requires little or no work to generate).

...Someone Else's Toothbrush

Complete your tax returns promptly.

Accept that someone will eventually stick either a magnet or a kid's drawing on the fridge. Once this happens it is only a matter of time before you can no longer see the fridge door.

Don't wait for something to happen, make it happen.

It's Never Okay to Borrow…

Everything matters but most things don't matter that much.

```
There's a fine line
between confidence
 and arrogance.
```

Own a paper shredder and shred any paperwork featuring personal details.

Don't judge people by their relatives.

...Someone Else's Toothbrush

Money spent on the right tools for a DIY job is never regretted.

Silence is sometimes the best answer.

Don't start a sentence if you don't know how you are going to finish it.

```
The first steps in
any venture are often
the toughest. Don't
give up too early.
```

It's Never Okay to Borrow…

If it was easy everyone would be doing it.

Processed cheese slices make for poor cheese on toast.

Take every opportunity you can because sometimes things only happen once.

Make big changes by first making small changes.

...Someone Else's Toothbrush

If you want to be perfect, start by making mistakes.

Man without a smile shouldn't open a shop.

Spend time and money making your garden a beautiful place to relax - it will repay you a hundredfold.

Always push your shopping trolley back to the trolley bay after unloading it.

It's Never Okay to Borrow…

You only really need two tools: WD-40 and duct tape. If it doesn't move and it should, use WD40. If it moves and it shouldn't, use duct tape.

Etiquette dictates that you should stand on the right-hand side of an escalator and leave the left clear for people to pass.

Engaging in confrontations with anyone online or in the real world will generally turn out to be a complete waste of time and effort.

...Someone Else's Toothbrush

If you send someone a birthday gift and they don't thank you, give them one more chance. If they do the same the following year, stop sending them gifts.

```
Make a friend of a
business partner but
don't make a business
partner of a friend.
```

Try not to moan too much - there'll be plenty of time for that when you are older.

It's Never Okay to Borrow…

The earlier you start thinking about your retirement plans, the earlier you will be able to retire.

Have a money box for loose change. Fill it up and then treat yourself with the contents.

Go where you are wanted.

...Someone Else's Toothbrush

Use notebooks to jot down thoughts, ideas and doodles and keep them to look at in years to come.

One of the greatest joys of having money is being able to give it away.

Don't remortgage your home to pay for day to day living expenses. If you can't afford your bills, earn more or spend less.

It's Never Okay to Borrow...

Ask older relatives to tell you stories from when they were younger.

Your life won't end just because you don't have the latest mobile phone.

Read anything by David Walliams.

```
   Flattery.
Smell it but don't
   swallow it.
```

...Someone Else's Toothbrush

Whatever you have, you'll always want more. Learn to be satisfied with less and save yourself the stress.

Negative people will pull you down. Positive people will lift you up. It's your choice.

Buy a decent pair of winter gloves and a scarf.

Learn to say, 'Sorry'.

It's Never Okay to Borrow…

When you bump into
someone who you
haven't seen for ages
and they say,
'Let's catch up soon,'
they don't mean it.

Women love and expect
surprise parties. Men don't
and would prefer that you
didn't bother.

Furniture superstore sales
never, ever end.

...Someone Else's Toothbrush

```
The right partner
will improve your
 life no end. The
wrong partner can
make it unbearable.
```

Read something by William Shakespeare.

If you have a meal with a group of friends, be happy to split the bill equally. Don't be the person who says, 'I only had...' and then goes on to calculate exactly what their meal cost.

It's Never Okay to Borrow…

Don't stick your nose into other people's business. Sometimes you just have to let them make their own mistakes.

```
It doesn't matter how
many Facebook friends
you have, you'll almost
  certainly be able to
count your real friends
      on one hand.
```

Have a signature dish that you can make without needing the recipe.

...Someone Else's Toothbrush

Girls: When talking to your friends, please don't call them 'Hun' or 'Babe'.

See if you can go a whole day without criticising anyone.

Karma is *always* watching.

4 GB is never enough.

It's Never Okay to Borrow…

It has never been known for someone to say, 'I wish that presentation/speech had been longer.'

If in doubt when going to an event, it's always better to be overdressed rather than underdressed.

If you are offered a glass of 'bubbly', you can be pretty sure it won't be champagne.

...Someone Else's Toothbrush

When sending a birthday card to someone you haven't seen for a long time, enclose a note.

Savour the moment because life is made up of moments.

When sending a message of thanks for a gift, personalise the message around the gift.

If you've enjoyed a book, recommend it to a friend.

It's Never Okay to Borrow…

You can't buy happiness but you can buy enjoyment.

If you are ever asked to be the best man, never say anything in your speech which would offend the oldest relative at the wedding.

When driving, if someone pulls in to let you pass, acknowledge your appreciation with a wave.

...Someone Else's Toothbrush

Enjoy a picnic every now and then.

Turning up 30 minutes early can be just as inconsiderate as turning up 30 minutes late.

Don't blame other people. Take responsibility.

Keep this book and add to it.

It's Never Okay to Borrow...

Don't argue with a fool. He will bring you down to his level and then beat you with experience.

Walk in the woods.

Put your phone/tablet down and talk.

If you become the boss, remember what it was like to be the trainee.

...Someone Else's Toothbrush

If a movie is remade, be sure to watch the original. It will almost certainly be better. Unless it's black and white, in which case it'll probably be rubbish!

Camp in a motorhome.

Do your supermarket shopping first thing in the morning or late in the evening. It'll be much quieter.

It's Never Okay to Borrow…

Know when you've lost the argument.

Don't hold grudges. Let it go.

```
Don't take advantage
 of someone else's
     generosity.
```

Above all else, make the most of life.

...Someone Else's Toothbrush

Add your own tips below...

www.ingramcontent.com/pod-product-compliance
Lightning Source LLC
Chambersburg PA
CBHW052025290426
44112CB00014B/2374